49 Revolutions

Reggie Pickett

49 Revolutions
© 2020/2021 by Reggie Pickett

Published by Pickett-Fennell Group
Bowie, Maryland

All rights reserved. No part of this publication may be used or reproduced in any manner whatsoever without written permission by the publisher.

Manufactured in the United States of America.

ISBN: 978-1-7359988-1-7

Cover design and illustrations by Reggie Pickett

Additional text edits by Andre Johnson
Additional format consulting by Kevin Winters

Table of Contents

Pssst 1
Here I Come 2
The Gift of You 3
Sometimes We Win 4
Rising Again 5
Hope Still Speaks 6
What I Must Tell Myself 7
broken crayons 9
Illuminate Us 10
You Are 11
Midnight Homilies 13
Will We Ever 14
Chit Chatting with God #1 15
Let Faith Breathe 17
God Is… 18
Recourse 19
Recovery 20
Yahushua's (Jesus) Praise! 21
Composition of Israel and New Breed 23
Just to Thank You 25
Safe Faith 26

Willie Lynch and Jesus	27
Chit chatting with God #2	28
The Panther of Boseman	29
Announcing John Lewis' Arrival	30
The Off Key Song	31
The Dread	34
Teach	36
Rotten Orange	38
What Matters?	39
In Great America	40
Boys of the Hood Revelations	42
I See Hope For Us, Black Man	43
chit chatting with God #3	44
In Other Folk's Box	45
Imprisoned Thoughts	46
Tired Words	47
rest eludes	48
Check Up	49
Lost and Found	50
The Day We Missed	51
No better day	52
Truth of Aged Wisdom	53

Prepared?	54
Non-Negotiable	55
Cause or Effect?	56
Any/Everything Equals Nothing	57
The Life Unfulfilled	59
Potential	60
The Bastard From Landover	61
what i need a father for?	63
Apology of a Tortured Soul	64
The Purple Mantle	65
chit chatting with God #4	66
The Must!	67
Remember This Son	69
Grab the Dog	70
Super	71
Always mom	72
I Love That You	73
Chit chatting with God #5	74
Natural Contributions	75
Mural of the Sky	76
When the Storm Ends	77
cultivating	78

Spin the Wheel	79
Word	80
Go	81
Haiku's	83
Natalie	92
Of My Sister Zandi (Resting with God)	93
Notes:	94

# 49 Revolutions

Pssst….

Hey you there…
You reading this

You can make it
You can do it
You can achieve it
You can still win

You can recover
You can get past it
Get after it
Age don't matter
You can still begin

You can still call on God
You still have a voice in the matter
He's still answering
And there can still be happily ever after

here I come

        here

...in this chaotic maze weighed
down by rigged rules and shackled
wages while being hunted by blue
snakes and cowards in white
collars that pull over to
white hoods

        i

...find ways to circumvent this
hurricane jungle going from hunted to hunter turning traps to
treasures while laying the foundation of a milk and honey
landscape

        come

...and see where the seed is watered
in the mist of desert level drought
and regeneration is as common
as monday. where we fly on
new wind and welcome the
idea of devouring the fruit
of today.

The Gift of You

if
what you have to give
can lift
the next man to live
in his
best adjective
your gift
is life givin'
as it is
and one
Yah is
truly happy with

Sometimes We Win

sometimes we lose
sometimes we function confused
left bruised
by the fustigation and abuse
sometimes we just lose

sometimes we fall
tripped up by nothing at all
but if you recall
pride was there first
and what hurts the worse
is we flirted with it all

…but sometimes we win
more often than we think …we win
even with things on the brink
and it seems we're gonna sink
in the blink of an eye
…we win

Rising Again

buried my greatness deep
      but my resurrection's here
      comin' out this cave
      drying the tears

and while I rise, I will fill my tomb
with 49 years
worth of all my fears and gloom.

Hope Still Speaks

And hope says

maybe everything negative
we have ever experienced
can be rearranged.

maybe the pain we feel will bow
to the notion of change

maybe in a new way of thought
a triumph can still be claimed

maybe if we believe and held our faith
our space can be obtained

maybe the events of a new day
can erase the paint of shame

and maybe just maybe
we will remember that love
shall ever reign.

What I Must Tell Myself

don't know if we would call this poetry
though my hope is we would know the potency
of our own voices spoken
even if they don't notice me
keep speakin' hope in the broken,
locked up spirits that need to be opened
the quiet soul knows when
it has something to say
i know
cause i'm the quiet soul at the bottom of the totem pole
wishing to be heard, wishing to be known
wishing my work was observed
wishing my art and my words weren't stuck in the hole
…the hole of the abyss so when i run amiss
i gotta speak a seed, i gotta speak life to my peace
i gotta speak vitality to my belief
i gotta speak breath so i can breathe
and accept what i receive and be the best i can be
and let God rise in me so none of this will die in me
must release all that lies in me
no matter how much society despises me
i'll keep on reminding me
that somebody out there is inspired by me
so decisively
i choose to view the vision of living
and fighting, and contributing to life and then
fight again to secure my win
so my purpose is alive when
i contrive the method of my survival
and my successful arrival and my impact wherever i go
now i'm staring down my revival
…i know
his hand is drafting my path

& i'm laughin at how he's kicking the devil's
(ha ha)
…derriere he's forever there on my behalf
i'm forever grateful i been able to outlast
being an outcast and i'm about past
due
so i will continue to pursue the menu of my virtue
through faith in what i seen him do
and all that i been through tells me i must continue
seeking to fulfil my potential
and embody all i was meant to
because god says i believe in you
if only you knew how powerful
the power in you is mediocrity would not be allowable
God says live my child with hope in me
than you will know and see
the beauty of you is indeed pure poetry!

broken crayons

mishandled, misused,
snapped in the middle
broken and abused,
stripped of covering
lost in a lonely place
seems a normal suffering
for us seemingly so easy to replace

yet we,
wherever we fall
leave a mark of notice
our presence is recorded
to our purpose we remain focused
devoted though they broke us
though they throw us away
though they drop us
without conscious
this one thing will always remain
no matter what broken part of me
you choose to pick up

…i'll always make beautiful color
'til i'm all used up.

because broken crayons
still color

Illuminate Us

you're a beautiful color
bright, sharp and bold
when you allow
the light to hit you
and bounce off
you
as a blessing
to others

you're bland and dull
and lifeless,
colorless
when hidden
in the shadows
void of the light

come out and
illuminate us.

You Are

you are
the manifestation of a thought in the creators mind.
you are formed as of his kind.
you are the thing he gave specific
attention to without distraction.
you are his passion
at that moment of eternal presence.
you are his action,
the very action to which he gave deference.
you are the only cross-reference
between you and God that will ever live.
you are the example God gives
of his love definitive.
you are a gift given.
you are what should've been
but when sin hit
he shifted
so now you are the object of his mission.
you are still the focus of his vision.
you are still the hope the world is missing.
you are the chosen.
you are a seed that will grow when
planted, protected, through rain and snow and
heat flows from you even when frozen.
you are what sprouted
in the middle of the impossible.
you are the envy of those that doubted.
you are the possible,
beloved like the prodigal
you are unstoppable
so astronomical
you are phenomenal
you are to know

so you can go
be who you are
you are impact, in fact
you are an institution
through your contribution
you are the solution
you are the certitude in confusion
you are the evidence to draw the conclusion
even though you are an illusion
…you'll get that later
you are a vision of beauty to our creator
you are all that!

Midnight Homilies

midnight once spoke of
amazing dreams
and possibilities
and a guiding light

>in a sea of darkness
>saying hold on
>to the hope of
>day break.

then one day
broke and burned its
peace to fine ashes
and sapped the life
out of all life-giving entities.
>…scorching hopelessness.

>>but the funniest of things
>>happened… midnight came
>>again with the reassuring
>>declaration that ash morphs
>>into beautiful glass and
>>rock and sits majestic

and high on a mountain. one
terribly torrid day can't kill
the hope day break brings
on a daily basis. you never
know how amazing dreams
and possibilities will surface.

Will We Ever

We have almost tried it all
And still we fall

We keep the search open
In hopes of mending the broken

We're sending messages
That match not the lessons we live

We talk about it cheaply
But talk only, just wounds us deeply

We need a strategy a new
The thing we know of ...but just won't do

Will we ever try to rise above
Will we ever fly on the wings of love

Chit Chatting with God #1

me:
most high, i'm not
looking to fail, i wanna
find great success.

God:
well my son, great success
is often found in places
we don't want to look.

Let Faith Breathe

let faith breathe
in the face of doubt
to give you the power
to move the mount

mountains that only God can move
so he can truly be glorified through

the faith you give
the faith you cultivate
that's the faith He gave
that's the faith that motivates

that's the faith that resuscitates
a life unlived
it's the kind that makes him say
I forgive

inhale a hope, exhale strength,
so I can truly see what He's giving me
inhale belief and exhale the results
of all that burst of creativity

and you'll find the refreshing wind,
flowing into a redeeming courage

to stop suffocating the dreams
and start seeing them flourish

God Is...

God is so indescribably awesome
beyond what words can say

God is undeniably beautiful
beyond what a master painter could paint

God stretches to depths unfathomable
he can reach us in our deepest hole

God is the love we seek,
the answer we need
he is the source to satisfy the soul.

Recourse

wonder why i struggle and strain
to comprehend the voice of
the one i'm connected to
when there is so much
your spirit has to convey
so much for me to do.

or is the problem not the voice
or the message, but the lesson
protruding through the noise of doubt
so we play doltish and dull-witted
pretending as if we don't get it
so we can live in a cloud.

for its easy to dwell in
a state of the unknown
for there is no work required
but this leads to a plethora of
days of empty blessings
such the life of unfulfilled desires.

it behooves me to figure the
translation and the correlation
or reconnect with the source
for the struggle and strain
drains the energy in me
…thank God he's my recourse.

Recovery

The theme ...recovery
Where I rediscover me
Cause this will bring my recovery
And free me loose from the other me
The other me
That smoothers me
The other me
That don't know how to love me
Thank God my full recovery
Is coming from above me
A lovely
Repaint...
More than a touch up
I'm redone utterly
Totally...
I'm a must see
It must be
His love for me
That makes a masterpiece of me
Devil can't crush me
Because the blood covered me,
He covers me
Leading the charge to my full recovery

Yahushua's (Jesus) Praise!

See my need to praise Him
Indeed my spirit bleeds it craves Him
From sin I'm free 'cause He gave Him
For me eternity's peace is based in Him
What's my need to place my faith in Him
It's by His grace I draw safe in Him
In Him, myself I've overcome
The self-destruction I know I've done
His reconstruction of my soul's begun
When He let them bang nails in 'em

Vision the blood stains wipe away
My mistakes, pains and the things I can't pay
My life was gained on that day
He overcame my cold dingy grave
Gave me power and said
My sins deleted this hour, I aint dead
You live with power
When the love you live you spread
Be my people's flower
I should smell of His scent
For its Him you represent

So I praise Him for the deliverance
The forgiveness of the mess I did
The willingness of Him to clear my debt
Cuz all of this was done at His expense

The drunkenness…paid
The lust…paid
The lack of trust…paid
For the stolen stuff…paid
Even the stuff

I can't speak of
…paid through His love
Made by His love, saved by His blood
Healed by His cuts
My new life revealed by word of His love

Will you listen to His love
For in His love I worship Him
Hence this is why my praise is all for Him

Composition of Israel and New Breed

I am not forgotten
For He knows my name
Must be a friend of God
Who else would keep
Chasing me down
Trading my sorrows
For overflow

I call you Jesus
And stand speechless
With lifted hands
I exalt thee
For your presence is heaven
And you've won my affection
So here I am to worship
Under African skies

Covered in Asia
With you at the center
It's raining
In this new season
I hear the sound
Singing it's not over
Turn it around
Can't you taste
The favor of the Lord
Rise within us

You are Alpha and Omega,
Holy,
My strength…
Surely and simplistically
You are good
Giving me a medley of praise

And I rejoice and rejoice
In the goodness and mercy
Following me
Where only one thing remains to do
Rejoice
Again I say rejoice

Just to Thank You

Peace you give my heart
When confusion wants to stay
You warm me with your presence
Launching strength to face the day.

I need your love, I need you to breathe
I need your comfort, I need your peace.
I need your hand to guide my way
So I stand, to give you all my praise.

Rose of Sharon, wonderful counselor
Kings of kings, source of love
Prince of peace, you are my peace
You died for me, just because

And I'm thankful, so very thankful
You save me daily, I just want to thank you

Safe Faith

Took the safe route
With predictable outcomes
And a capped ceiling

Like living in a cage
toiling like slaves
For a breakthrough that never came

Even thought God was pleased
For hunting the idea of being holy
Sparked by the dark need to be somebody

It's the illusion of religion

Empty faith can only lead
To places where fences trap you in
and feed you frustration

But something is out there
Beyond this gate of security
Waiting to be claimed

And the safe faith will never see this place
Or please the God of heaven
For the safe route is not the route of faith
It's the home of oppression.

Willie Lynch and Jesus

As nice as you are
There is still
Someone out there
That hates you
To death

On the contrary

As flawed as you are
There is someone
That loves you
Enough to
Die for you

Chit chatting with God #2

Me:
what if they don't think I have what it takes? What if they don't like my ideas? What if they say I'm not qualified? What if they don't approve of me? What if they...

God:
hush... you don't need man's approval when you have mine!

The Panther of Boseman

Black, graceful and strong, young, gifted and black, fearless and fierce a panther is.
Symbol of culture and advance, cunning intelligence a king with purpose.

The judge, king of soul, American pastime pioneer to king of Wakanda with wisdom molded at the mecca of Howard U to navigate the powerful stories of the powerful.

Forever iconic to the mission of the revolution that is not being televised but filmed for cinema and social media.

You drank of the heart shaped herb to temper the internal growth that medicine has little control of yet it was the creator, the father that provided the cure in a way unexpected.

The black panther king now rests beside the Ziziphus Mucronata tree with the ancestors sharing stories of the prowl it takes to pounce on the prey of opportunity. Purpose fulfilled, peace found, your hunt is complete.

Wakanda forever, king. Wakanda forever.

Announcing John Lewis' Arrival

I can imagine the gathering at the pearly gates when angels announced the arrival of John Lewis. Signs of job well done and balloons and poms and chants of you fought that fight soldier, you fought that fight.

the Off key Song

the ignorant
sound of the privileged
exists
and lives
in the melody
of a song off key
singing lyrics of why don't we
focus on
the real issues of the same ole song
because they don't want
to be made to face their wrong
though some play along
until
time to write the check
write the bill
repent and correct
or clean up their spill
they will
write a blanket statement
claim to make changes
yet things stay the same its
the way they play this game
with us
it's a shame but we must
exclaim we serious
or put flames to this hideous
ridiculous system
we live in.
i aint finished
don't wanna hear of this
what about black on black crime
when the system committed the high crime
and forced us through the pipe line

to prison and violence
by poisoning our bright minds
you forced the guidelines
on us
took our right minds from us
put us in slums and drugged us
gave us guns so slugs we bust
and you have the nerve to blame us
where we get the crack and heroine
what black american
had planes to fly back to central and south america
i don't hear ya
but here's more of
what you fear more of
sure nuff
its black men educated
so for our school placement
you make it
a place where
no creative space is
open for us to chase our greatness
how we gonna flourish
again it's our brains you seek to malnourish
again you claim
that our lack of test score gain
is on us.
seems you aint for us
but you know what
we still gonna thrive in this misery
still gonna find victory
…our delivery, spiritually
physically and mentally
that liberty
was meant for me
and we
was meant to see
the unlocked mystery of our history
it will be

positively
beautiful
transmutable
to human gold
simply musical
and though you think i'm delusional
you should know
the pharmaceutical
anecdote
i hold
is love
and that's the missing note
the missing chord
to your off key song

The Dread

Imagine if I said you
Can't get a bag of Skittles
Or jog in your neighborhood
Or sleep in a bed
Drive at night
Shoot
Driving in daylight
For fear of being shot dead
Imagine living with that dread

The dread of a death
Sentence for a misdemeanor
Or a prison bid
For what someone
Else did corroborated
By a false witness
When a mass murderer
Is coddled and pampered
Having it his way
With Whoppers, a
Coke and large fries
Yet if I did it
I'd be dead twice
That's my dread

My dread gives
Soil to expanded
Crow's feet and
Gray hairs and
Stress line marks
Traced by the worry
Of will I come home
To make sure

My sons come
Home or how will
They fair in a world
That don't care and
Wants to suffocate
Them in the most
Brutal kind of way.

Dread is a terrible
Way to live

Teach

parents can't teach
or pass "right" along
because society is woefully wicked
and dead wrong

school system
has hidden slave curriculum
that aint all that hidden
especially in inner city conditions
the mission
…graduate our children to prison
get'em a masters in 'disastrous livin'
phd as a societal villain
the dissertation was written
title given
'niggers, how we gonna kill 'em'
but i aint willin'

so let's change the narrative
and teach 'em their heritage
and give our kids an inheritance
so they never live
in poverty conditions that never give
hope as a means that can ever live
in their atmosphere or environment.

so the struggle continues
in correcting our educational issues
build up our hbcu's
improve our schools
so the world sees you
in the value God sees in you
and in spite of all this i still believe in you.

so parents…
teach and pass 'right' along
even when society
is wicked and dead wrong.

Rotten Orange

seems like the golden rule
been overruled

for selfish gain

at the expense of humanity
it's sad to see

the sad try to hide their pain

let's hope
we don't hide our vote

with silent screams unheard

and something to say
but nothing fear lets us convey

and so complain of what's observed.

it leads to enslaved tears
and wasted years

symptoms of a contaminated soul

filthy of old fools
who discarded the golden rule

for the sake of being powerful

What Matters?

black lives matter
blue lives matter
all lives matter
blah blah blah

seemingly in this country
it's only the opinions
of the rich lives
…that matter

at least in 2020 all votes mattered

oh… and black lives DO matter!

In Great America

It's crazy the way they have tried to kill us black folk in great America.
>Take our mind, take our spirit, take our faith,
>Crush our belief, crush our families, chain us in unfamiliar space and whip and rape.
>Strip our names, maim our identity,
>Claim we are less than and primitive. Unintelligent, are the lies they spit.
>It's crazy the way they have tried to kill us black folk in great America.

I say it's crazy the way they have tried to kill us black folk in great America.
>Unfit conditions to live in
>Pickin' cotton and sellin our kids
>And feedin us rotten pigs.
>Gettin' rich on our backs, painting pain on our backs, making our ladies lay on their backs not even behind our backs with riffles digging holes in our backs.
>It's crazy the way they have tried to kill us black folk in great America.

Seriously yall, it's crazy the way they have tried to kill us black folk in great America.
>A system with no hope for me only ropes and trees and poverty
>And burning crosses and other atrocities
>Like locking me up for iniquitous policies.
>Police who shot me,
>Slammed me, planted contraband and narcotic on me,
>Squeeze the breath from me with knees on my neck, and I'm screaming i can't breathe while reaching out for my mommy.

It's crazy the way they have tried to kill us black folk in great America.

Do you understand how crazy it is the way they have tried to kill us black folk in great America.
    Poisoned by syphilis – Tuskegee, poisoned by not giving us the meds we needed when were sick as a slick and easy way to kill us.
    Poisoned by liquor, to kill the thought process,
    Poisoned by an uninspired educational system full of lies, poisoned by cooked cocaine cooking up a suppressed brain and the nation watches us go insane in so many ways.
    Poisoned with HIV/Aids,
    Poisoned by the great taste of sugar and salt,
    Diabetes and stress to bring our hearts to a halt.
    Poisoned with cancer
    And the so-called answer
    For treatment, how convenient
    For the medical industry's bottom line
    …while folks out here dyin'.
    Poisoned in 2020 with covid-19 and an idiot at the helm tellin' us everything is just great here in the states of great America.

I'm tellin yall, it's just crazy the way they have tried to kill us black folk here in great America.

boys of the hood revelations

aint wanna sell no drugs, poison the community, resort to violent measures,

aint wanna derail the youngin's,
drain the hope, assist the system in becoming a suppressor

and i definitely
don't wanna reside in your rotten prisons
and live in a den of attrition

yet need drives the mission and validates the reason we do what we don't really wanna do to do the thing we need to

you see

we just wanted to eat and have a safe space to sleep

I See Hope For Us, Black Man

black man
black man

our path has been tumultuous
for satan sought our soul to crush
but he aint know the force
that flows over us

so we continue to overcome
by the hand of Jehovah's love
my inner man smiles
for i still see hope for us

black man
black man
i see hope for us.

chit chatting with God #3

me:
look God I don't understand, I'm trying to figure this thing out 'cause I just need to know it all. Can't you just make it clear for me.

God:
Regg, you not always gonna know where I'm taking you or what I'm doing with your life. Just trust in me with all you got, deep in your soul, don't rely on your own wisdom. Check for me in everything you do and I will lead you down your path like I said in Proverbs 3:5&6 to be exact.

Me:
So… where we going??

God: (face in hand shaking his head)
Will he ever learn

in other folk's box

it's hard sometimes
to please everyone
as the job description
seems to require
of me.

apparently one needs
faith to please
and they put more faith in me
than i can see

i owe it to them to find
what they all seem to know
is present

so they can find fulfillment
and meaning in my very existence.

now how that sound??

Imprisoned Thoughts

my thoughts
beseech my conscious
to set them free
      so they can insert themselves
      into the soil of life,
      take root and bloom

but so often they're suffocated
by the idea that
freedom will
only sentence them to death

...so my conscious keeps them imprisoned

Tired Words

the words are running
wild in my head
blurting out
desperate sounds
that stand alone,
lost and lonely
and exhausted
because
the attention
they seek
they crave
they desire
can't respond
for the world
they live in
lay in a
dream
filled
dead
sleep.

rest eludes

laid down to rest
looked forward to pleasant dreams
listened to the sheep babble
lined up like prisoners in
school hallways
legitimized my anxiety
liberated its compadre…
stress
let 'em roam freely about
lounging on a bed of
pillow cloud
lost
that rest i was looking forward to
labored to find it as the time flew
lamp came on gradually brightening the room
lest i realized night and day lapped me
…and rest still eludes

Check Up

doctor said
i give you
five years

    ...20 years ago

guess he didn't know
heavens diagnosis
or treatment plan and
the angels hope for
my strength to endure
this illness was far more
formidable than
five measly years.

in check-ups today

doctor says
keep doing
what you do
now realizing he
don't have a say
or years to give.

but now he knows who does

Lost and Found

Thinking I was lost
I searched to be found
but once found
I found myself
Lost again.

Thought I was found
While walking around lost
But now realizing
being lost is the
only way I will
ever be
Found.

The Day We Missed

one day turns to another
and another turns to years
and one day the phone rings
or the text buzzes
only to hear
such and such passed away
didn't we speak just the other day

…oh wait
Must've missed a day

and then you realize that
one day turns to another
and another turns to years
and we wonder where did it all go
and why hadn't we stopped to see
that day that turns into another
that turns to years

that's the day we missed.

No better day

Yesterday was full of flaws and mistakes, wasted opportunities and unsaid prayers …and dreams left in slumber.

Tomorrow is schizophrenic, moody and unreliable. It might show up, it might not. And if it shows, you don't know if it's bringing problems, monsters and nightmares or if it's carrying blessings and treasures. You never know what to expect from tomorrow.
…Totally undependable.

But Today though…
There's no better day than Today. Today is always ready to make something happen.

Truth of Aged Wisdom

So many

      lessons I've
      taught over the
      years and yet…

            I've surmised that
            I haven't learned

                  a single
                  thing.

Prepared?

Whatcha gonna do
when the dam breaks
and you can't swim?

Non-Negotiable

Success don't care
>what you feel like doing.

What it requires
>is its only concern

do we have a deal?

Cause or Effect?

Call it arrogance
but I hate it when
I don't know the answer
for the cause
of the pain you're in

or am I the cause of your pain
..would make sense
since I struggle
to fix me

Any/Everything Equals Nothing

I wanted to be a great artist
Impactful like Jacob Lawrence
Jean Michel Basquiat
And van Gogh
Creating art that
Arrests the eye
And issues the pupil
A life sentence.

I wanted to be a great poet
Impactful like Langston
Hughes and Maya Angelou
Writing verses that
Make the soul to
Caress its intelligence

I wanted to be a great communicator
Impactful like Jim
Vance, Melvin Lindsey,
Malcolm X and Dr. King
Hosting shows and interviews
And giving speeches that inspire
The spirit

I wanted to be a great song writer
Impactful like Stevie the Wonder,
Smokey, Face, Paul McCartney
And Rakim, Bob Marley,
Penning lyrics that
Make the eardrum strum

I wanted to be great chess player
Impactful like Maurice Ashley
And Bobby Fisher

Outwitting the most
Strategic of brains

I wanted to be great at everything
But everything feasts on action
Depleting the energy
For acting on anything
Wherefore nothing becomes the outcome
And I remain the unimpactful
One full of talent and impact
That still needs to be spilled.

But now I just want help to go to sleep!

The Life Unfulfilled

had so much promise,
        had so much potential
had the desire
        and even had the skill

but the skill and potential
        never met with belief and faith
only believed the voice of fear and doubt
        so fear and doubt he chased

if he could only replace
the voice in his head
that said,
he can't do, when he could
        his life would have grew,
wild and free everywhere he stood

but he died suddenly,
and honestly no one cared
cause he never shared
what he had to the right people
but
…he did share
        but the wrong people
                are evil

even when they stand in holy positions
        …he didn't know his position,
                didn't understand his mission
                now.   …nobody will miss him

Potential

Great potential
Broken dreams
Potential rises again
More tears and screams
Potential boomerangs
Another fail it seems

…but potential don't die

So I won't deny
That eventually I
Will fight and exceed
Whatever potential
Ever meant for me.

The Bastard From Landover

When I was 8 years old a friend of mine kept speaking foreign words to me.
Words like father and daddy.

He said they were his.

Always saying my daddy this,
my father that.
Even said to me where your father at?
I don't know nothin' bout that father crap.

What that mean, where you get it from,
how I get one,
don't mean to sound dumb,

but I don't know these words.
These not words I've heard in my abode. These not words I've observed in my home.

Me, my,
daddy, father,

I don't know.
To me it's unusual.
Sounds cool though.
kinda cruel though.
I wonder if everyone in school know,
he said I think so,
cause they call you bastard, the bastard from Landover.
Bastard??
Another word I never heard of.

Who calls me that?

Ms. Beagle, Ms. Beard, and Mr. Womack.
Oh crap,

that's the teachers.
Gotta find out what that word means. Looked it up said that sounds kind a mean. I looked up, that's what they think of me.

No wonder I am in the lowest reading group at a school that aint even in my district.

My mom wanted me to get educated at one of them good schools out the way.
So I'd be safe.
Cause the place we stayed was cray.
Had to watch everything when I went out to play.
Anyway,

so I'm the bastard from landover, labeled and grouped
not being able to show what I'm able to do though I'm capable
but now I'm hatin' school.
Don't even know if my mom ever knew
what I was going through.

…But at least my vocabulary grew.

what i need a father for?

i took a beaten after school one day so the hood started teaching me to fight,
>soon it wasn't no mo beatins'.

first eyed a girl the way a man eyes a woman …in the first grade,
>a predator was born.

started gambling my lunch money in the 5th grade,
>i can make money, take money, create money.

teacher said i would never be nothing, streets said you'll paint the sidewalk crimson,
>still here though after fighting both monsters.

they thought i was nice because i was quiet,
>i was plottin'

somebody said something about being responsible,
>so i learned how to guess …at times.

gifted, talented at a lot of things, where was joe jackson to coach it?
>eventually made something of myself.

none of this was any good though.
>i despised authority, authority always dropped my ball.

momma was there though, mama was authority enough, mama was tough, mama loved, mama prayed,
>God listened…

i once asked God, what i need a father for?

>i think He cried because i just didn't get it.

Apology of a Tortured Soul

I've done so much to cause grief
In the sight of God.

Enough to send straight to hell
Without second thought.

Planted seeds of pain and became the vein
That hardened and broke hearts.

I have messed up so much I don't even know
The full ramifications of it all.

Don't know why God's hand chose to bless me and kept me even still guarded

When so often it was his way, his law, his love
I disregarded

I'm sorry though, I apologize, sincerely
Yet repenting is sometimes a struggle

But I'm pushing forward. So grateful God's grace is full enough to ease the tortured soul

The Purple Mantle

I wear purple as a reminder
of my kingship
Accented with gold
for the blessings run deep

Ever learning through obstacles
a rising phoenix I am
But I rise not
without extending my hand

This movement may produce
a friend from the ashes
Transcending the divide of
Thought and social class

until a leader emerges
fierce as a K-9
hunting to save lives
who in turn will save mine

see I've been wounded
while trying to navigate this struggle
at times doubtful but I'm reminded
my mantle is still purple.

chit chatting with God #4

God:
Ok son, now let's try this again. When I say you can get up and you can do this and that and there really are still blessings for you and much fruit for you to bare and there is still enough fight left in you to win… you should SIMPLY say …what??

Me:
Yes Sir

God:
Ok than… stop going back and forth with me, say 'yes Sir' and go realize my TRUTH for you!

The Must!

surrounded by three boys who look of me
and who look to me
to direct what they could be
they make me refocus on what i should be
their development consumes me
                      as it should

              …see

i purpose to listen
intently discipline
pray wisdom to give'em
shine life as their eyes glisten
       at night i kiss'em
paternal protection the mission

a man must stay prayed up
cause they must be raised up
              by their father's strength
pops are you strong enough
can they thrive off of
              what you bring

hope those three boys know
the love i hold
gotta make sure it shows
fight harder for their gold
rise early gentlemen to assure their purpose unfolds
it's on us to know
gentlemen it's on your counsel
the responsibility is real,
none much greater
lord we seek you still,

we seek you greater
father you lead us
as fathers we need you
we give you complete trust
cause as fathers,
having you as father is indeed the must!

Remember This Son

Listen young man
to what I'm telling you. For

you are more than a state test score
used to fit you in a certain box of oppression. They

can't measure the heart that roars and pounds in the center of your
soul. They

won't understand the tenacious
desire you possess to use every

molecule of your fearfully
and wonderfully made being. It

don't matter how much they try to suppress you into their limited
vision of you and your life.

Don't
Don't you
Don't you ever
Don't you ever settle

For anything less than god's plan.
Ever. You always fight for you.

Grab the Dog

A father stresses upon
his young son to not be
so timid with the dog. 'Grab
him with confidence as if
you are in full control.'

*'But dad when i reach to grab
him he snaps and bites and
his teeth are sharp and hurt.'*

'No son, there is no other way
to handle an adversary than
with intentional confidence
with your confrontation,
determined and in control.'

Water filled the boy's eyes he replies, *'but
dad it really hurts when he bites me.'*

With the stern look of a
father piercing through
is son's soul, 'yeah son, I
know it's gonna hurt,
sometimes it'll hurt bad but
the sooner you realize
the levels of pain it can
dish out the less it'll hurt.
No need for timidity son,
grab it to seize more control
over its attacks.'

Super

Superwoman,
Wonder woman,
Bat girl, that girl
Black girl magic
Oprah, Mrs. Obama,
Simone, Serena,
Natalie the wife of me,
My own mama,
Kamala, etc.,
Rise like the queen
Maya
Angelou
Phenomenal,
Ultra like powerful
Bloom beautiful
Like flowers do
You a true
Super hero
Hero is just how you do
Given the power to
Birth and nurture
Hold ya or hurt ya
If you try to hurt the
Thing she gives birth to
She's a wonder
Woman
Hero
Super

Always mom

Always been there
Always cared
Always concerned for my well being
Always a rock in my despair

Always a force of discipline
a source of wisdom
Always on a knee in prayer
For when I wouldn't listen

Always the example of strength
Picture of uncompromising love
Whether I was right or wrong
It never faltered, never gave up

Always the voice I hear
Always a lended ear
Always giving the need
Even of things I could not see

Always the jewel
That's always been there
I'm always in ma's heart
And I will Love always

I Love That You

I love that you like me
Enough to love me
Like I be
Something
Special
When you know
Where my skeletons rest
And where the nest is
Of my flaws I confess
And attempt to hide
In the closet of my stress
And in my mess
You can smell the filthy scent
Linger under the deodorant
Of a broken spirit
And still give me hope
Like I deserved it
I don't deserve this
But I heard its
What grace looks like
I love that
No matter what I look like
You still like to look at me
One day I hope you can look and see
That I too love the look of you and me.

Chit chatting with God #5

Me:
So I'm going to do this, and I'm going to go here, and I'm planning to do this, and I…

God:
LOL

Natural Contributions

I see you in skies
Of gray and blue
As clouds ride the wind
I can see you move

And birds sing melodies
Of your rich glory
Crickets chirp and blurt
Screams of you are worthy

Leaves dance free and
Liberated on tree branches
Unashamed and confident
As the green enhances

At night your audience
Stares in staunch formation
And frogs and crickets
Plead in buzzing ovation

Do it again god for life flourishes
In how you spin
But man gets dizzy though
…so we only contribute sin.

Mural of the Sky

A spot of blue
Peaking threw
    gray canvas
With black streaks
And clear pointed ovals
All over what can be seen.

But what you can't see
Is what is underneath
    the dreary color
You don't know
The undertone laid below
    the eerie cover

There's a bright ball
    of yellow with streaks
Spreading across a peaceful blue spread
The over lay
Of gray
    is only temporary
As it disappears
So whatever is real can appear again

When the Storm Ends

I find the sound of thunder peaceful
And rain drops melodic
Hypnotic whispers of wind speak
Of a relaxing flow of life
Saying slow down child
Slow down
Yet mind your attention
For this peace you feel
Is surrounded by
Violent storm
And crushing
Conditions
That will not
Be controlled
Or predicted
…inhale, exhale
Dwell in the calm
And listen
Closely
For the sound
Of silence
Will soon
Scream
Of chaos
Again.

cultivating

ever notice how
you can't get
good peaches
in winter?

you're juiciest
in your season

other seasons are
for nurturing
your roots!

Spin the Wheel

      In the deep
dark vast of
space where it
seems nothing can
live,

      there are
sparkles of light
and flourishing life
and a place
to impact the
direction of the
entire universe.

      spin
the wheel and
see where God
leads.

      Even in
The deep dark.

Word

Love
    Hope
        Faith
            Pray
                Praise
            Heal
        Redeemed
    Unity
Discipline
    Rise
        Persevere
            Fight
                Learn
                    Peace
                Give
            Joy
        Express
      Wisdom
Ancestors
      Forgive
          Apologize
              Observe
                  Think
              Strategize
          Act
      Try
Do
      Faith
          Hope
              Love

Go

With the pressure on
And a decision to make
And Dark paths looming
And a life at stake

So much unknown
But can't stay here
So much to unfold
Though frozen in fear

A prayer to utter
Before a dream to chase
a whiff of hope
now take a step of faith

Haiku's

American Black
slavery, prison
poverty, drugs and police
crushed yet we thrive still

American Black Folk
it pains me to see
the pain of people stolen
pain of people lost

Now You Hear Us
so now they want to
listen since we decided
to wreck the city

iPhone or Android
never would've thought
god would use a cell phone to
rescue a nation

Verbs
actions speak louder
empty statements to appease
let your words be verbs

inure
oppression the rule
black folk were inured to this
so fighting's easy

burnt sienna soul
sun painted beauty
a solid and strong sculpture
motherland marvel

your dismissed
my contributions
none ever contemplated
flush your opinion

student
don't always appear
like you can procure gain but
i believe in you

emancipated
aint a slave no mo
snatchin' down ya noose and ya
confederate flags

color
red yellow and blue
primary colors as light
merged, blinded to black

9/11
amazing sun rise
planes with distorted flight plans
disastrous day

worth
they won't want to pay
enough to meet the worth of
you… for you're worth blood

irony
brothers threw joseph
deep in a pit then sold him
into a life of power

the gallow
can't imagine the
pressure of the tree that held
the weight of eternal life

internal flames
felt the flame burn the
skin of my soul from the heat
of elohim's will

utopia
looked over the hill
at the foot of heaven. i'm
too awe struck to speak

grace
choices of folly
one right after another
but you still love me

perspective
angry clouds above
hurricane winds crush the land
yet the sun still shines

live
look through the window
don't you see life happening
so why stay inside

french quarter hope
new orleans never
missed a marti gras after
katrina, why? …hope

found lost
been waiting for god
gods been waiting for me too
found him, i was lost

beauty spoken
a picture is worth
a thousand words, if words say
something worth seeing

vision
sight ahead of time
to tell actions where to go
or action won't budge

carelessness
a slip of the hand
drops and shatters face of phone
like uncared for dreams

van God the artist
the paintings of god
masterpieces stretched across
eternal canvas

purity
preserve the strength found
in a purple heart by the
taste of virgin salt

past problem
what happens to the
insects that bug you in their
season long gone

snow
a blanket covers
my earths bed of soiled riches
and cleanses the air

sunrise
from black to bluish
pink, the bright white bail appears
night's silence lifted

tears
rain drops hit my cheeks
leave trails of ash. refreshing
rain   ...or are these tears?

flavor of life
unique shapes of snow
flakes settle on the hills as
salt seasons the bland

fool's
why must we live of
animals rules unruly
yet we look the fool

forever in a minute
it's been a minute
been a year plus a minute
but not 2 minutes

fantasy island
fantasy island
i long to spend the summer
winter, spring and fall

my autobiography
thinking, risk taker
who sees the world's great beauty
artist i shall be

once loco
the wild child running
tame. once wild as a zebra
chasing starved lions.

the worst enemy
the enemy strikes
must be destroyed or suffer
but that's suicide

new me
quarantined thoughts bloom
now bees seek my sweet nectar
i'm a fresh new herb

interests
this, that, many thoughts
always all over the place
my life is abstract

filth
destined for greatness
a life of riches and glut
but i aint show up

Natalie

wither
if i cease to bloom
like flowers in the winter
you have gone adrift

love's journey
walk with me on white
water pure as pearls untouched
wilt with me my dear

air
i breathe without thought
for my secret space you fill
my air you must be

time stand still
i shudder to think
my life less you, so i delve
suspended in now

Natalie
when God made woman
and envisioned my soul's rib
his thoughts were of you

Of My Sister Zandi (Resting with God)

9/11 10 years later
your dream was cut short
with a nightmare of sad truth
rest now in heaven

hello, may i speak to Zandi
Heaven called for you
In the mist of summer's end
been cold ever since

she's flying in rainbows
Most beautiful soul
fiery passion and grit
soaring through rainbows

Notes:

Natalie

You are sooooooo amazing, beautiful, and strong. A true gift from God. I am favored indeed. There is so much in you that must come out. Let nothing stop you. Ever! You are an answer to prayers I didn't even know I needed to prayer.

Mom

Everything I know about hard work, sacrifice, perseverance, love, loyalty, strength and toughness, I learned from you. I would be the weakest of men if it were not for you. Thank you for loving me, even when it was hard, no matter the circumstance. Forever grateful.

To my 3 sons

In case I haven't told you these things you need to know, you can read them regularly.

You are becoming incredibly special young men.

You must trust and follow God. Good faith will move mountains.
Treat people right.
Always look out for each other. Don't drift away from each other.
Love, Love, Love
Learn as much as you can. Be lovers of learning.
Work hard as you can than work a little harder. DO NOT BE LAZY!!!! Lazy will get you a reservation on a street corner bench.
Always take care of your mama
Make wise decisions especially with your money, women and friends. Read Proverbs regularly. None of you are built for any type of imprisonment.

Good friendship is essential to the soul. (Thank you Omega Psi Phi Fraternity, Inc.)
Never give up on your dreams. Don't spend more time building someone else's dream than your own.
Find YOUR God given gift, talent, passion and work it, work it, work it, for God's glory. You will add value to others and yourselves.
Don't get caught up with a woman you can't trust.
Don't be in a rush to have sex. I know that will be hard but it's a trap. Wait for your wife.
You will have times in your life when you will be scared but do not let fear run your life. You must learn to overcome fear. You must learn to protect yourselves.
It's hard being a black man in America. Learn the struggle and overcome it. You come from strong families and a strong people. Fight for what is right.
Pray often, be thankful, laugh and cry. It will cleanse your soul. What would Yahushua (Jesus) do?? Read your Bible and you will know.

Reggie: You are a leader, problem solver, clever, and smart. Let it come out. Develop it. Have a winning mindset (even if it looks like you are losing) and you will win.

Reese: You are a leader, hard worker, driven, smart and caring. I wish I had your drive. Don't let no one tell you, you can't... You can!

Ramsey: You are a leader, strong personality, smart, and observant. Focus, focus, focus. Work, work, work.

All 3 of you are amazing in your own ways. Creative in your own ways. Brilliant in your own ways. Use Godly wisdom and find out just how much.

I love you all always,

Dad (Daddy-Reese calls me Daddy)